目录

编辑　拉萨市旅游局
北京市旅游局
制作　旅游杂志社
编委会委员　于长江 德吉卓嘎 熊玉梅 温子吉 顾晓园 扎西江村
封面题字　洛桑江村
主编　王军
责任编辑　龚威健
撰稿　黄良端 杨如军
翻译　闫军红　王建华　崔薇　刘小妹
摄影　赵燕平　土登　觉果　旺久　龚威健　杜宏　格桑达瓦
巴桑次仁

图书在版编目（CIP）数据

拉萨旅游指南／拉萨市旅游局，北京市旅游局编.
北京：中国旅游出版社，2001.10
ISBN 7-5032-1911-4

Ⅰ.拉…　Ⅱ.①拉…　②北…　Ⅲ.旅游指南－拉萨市　Ⅳ.K928.975.1

中国版本图书馆 CIP 数据核字(2001)第 078190 号

拉萨旅游指南
出版发行：中国旅游出版社
地址:北京建国门内大街甲九号
邮编：100005
电话：010-65201011
印刷：北京国彩印刷有限公司
版次：2001 年 10 月第 1 版
印次：2001 年 10 月第 1 版第 1 次
开本：787x1092mm　1/32
印张：2　001600

拉萨—西藏自治区的首府，是西藏政治、经济、文化的中心和交通枢纽；也是藏传佛教的圣地，世界文化名城，中国优秀旅游城市之一；也是一个充满生机与活力的正向现代化迈进的古城。

地理位置

拉萨，位于西藏中南偏东部，雅鲁藏布江支流——拉萨河北岸的河谷平原上，东经91度零6分，北纬29度36分，跨距277公里，周围与四个地区11个县接壤，是我国西南边陲一座较大的高原城市。

地形地貌

拉萨地域辽阔，地形、地貌复杂多样，平均海拔3658米，总面积三万平方公里。新建城区51.4平方公里。最北边是藏南与藏北的结合地带，海拔在4200至4900米之间，山丘起伏，有着众多的天然草场。西藏最大的咸水湖——纳木湖，即位于拉萨境内。念青唐古拉山位于该市西北喜马拉雅山东麓。海拔5000多米，峰峦逶迤，气候宜人。是极佳的游览圣地。

自然资源

拉萨自然条件独特，地质地貌复杂，这些自然条件赋予了拉萨丰富的旅游资源。在三万平方公里的土地上，河流纵横，水力资源潜力巨大，连绵的雪山峡谷和高原蕴藏着丰富的矿产。辽阔的当雄草原、奇特的地热温泉、肥沃的河谷平原、品种繁多的动植物资源，使拉萨成为高原上一块美丽富饶的地方。

气 候

拉萨，山环水绕，气候清爽宜人，最高气温28℃，最低气温-14℃，平均气温8℃，降雨集中于7、8、9月，年降雨量500毫米左右。年日照时间长达3000小时以上，素有“日光城”之誉，也是盛夏难得的避暑圣地。

历 史

拉萨，藏语意为“圣地”，其历史可追溯到一千三百多年前。公元7世纪，松赞干布统一西藏，迁都惹萨（今拉萨），当时这里还是一片沼泽地。松赞干布在红山上兴建了宫殿（即今布达拉宫前身），后相继建成了大昭寺、小昭寺，高原古城逐渐形成。拉萨于1951年和平解放，1960年设市，现辖七县一区，即：堆龙德庆县、当雄县、尼木县、曲水县、达孜县、墨竹工卡县、林周县和城关区。

人口与民族

拉萨市人口48万，其中市区人口20万左右，有藏、汉、回等31个民族，藏族人口占89.7%。

科 技

拉萨的科技管理工作开始于20世纪70年代。20多年来，全市共建科技机构近20个，各级各类专业科技人员六千多名，推动了全市科技的发展。

教 育

解放前，拉萨没有一所正规学校。西藏和平解放50年来，拉萨的教育事业从无到有，从小到大，逐步走上协调、稳步、持续、发展的道路。全市共有各级各类学校五百多所，在校学生七万多人，已建成从幼儿教育、中小学教育、中等职业教育到普通高等教育比较完整的体系.

园林绿化

拉萨城市绿化面积约1360公顷，覆盖率达32%，公共绿化面积109.68公顷，人均占有绿化面积12平方米，居全国前列 。

组织机构

拉萨市人民代表大会及其常务委员会是全市国家权利机关。其作用是：审议、决定全市的一些重大问题；对法律及政府、法院、检察院的工作实施监督；行使选举和任免权以及监督权、决定权、立法权。工作逐步法制化、制度化、规范化。

拉萨市人民政府

拉萨市人民政府是拉萨市人民代表大会的执行机关和行政机构。受自治区政府直接领导，统辖全市日常行政工作。

对外关系

1980年以来，拉萨市加大改革开放的力度，促进横向经济联合，加强经济技术交流与合作，招商引资工作取得了较好成绩。目前，拉萨市已与拉美地区的2个城市建立了国际“友好城市”关系。

TRAVEL TIPS 旅游知识

进藏手续

若您计划到西藏拉萨市进行观光游览或考察访问，请向拉萨市人民政府外事办公室、拉萨市旅游局垂询。

由于目前西藏旅游的交通基础设施、接待能力及藏民民族文化传统、文物古迹和自然环境保护等诸多原因，政府鼓励发展团体旅游。所有进藏旅游、探亲、参观访问、学习或进行商贸活动工作的外国友人必须办理进藏确认函。

联系电话：0891-6324691
　　　　　6323632

进藏确认函：凡有组织的海外旅行团队进藏旅游，西藏任何一家旅游社均可办理进藏确认手续。

拉萨办事处

地址：拉萨市藏医院路4号雪域旅馆二楼

电话：0891-6349239

西藏旅游局驻北京办事处

电话:010－65936538

传真:010-65035802

西藏旅游局驻香港办事处

电话:0852-29221028

传真:0852-25276337

西藏旅游局驻成都办事处

电话:028-3401807

传真:028-3401807

西藏旅游局驻上海办事处

电话:020-62748488

传真:020-63211016

西藏旅游局驻西安办事处

电话:029-7815987

传真:029-7815987

西藏旅游局驻格尔木办事处

电话:0979-4835321

传真:0979-4835321

西藏旅游局驻尼泊尔办事处

电话:00977-1420964

传真:00977-1422758

西藏旅游局驻日本办事处

电话:003-36393119

传真:003-36393896

西藏旅游局驻美国办事处

电话:001-9096298888

传真:001-9096298889

西藏旅游局驻广州办事处

电话: 020-81099136

传真: 020-81099136

西藏旅游局驻重庆办事处

电话: 023-65302750

传真: 023-65302750

西藏旅游局驻大连办事处

电话: 0411-2646283

传真: 0411-2646252

西藏旅游局驻云南办事处

电话: 0887-8229028

传真: 0887-8229028

西藏旅游局驻深圳办事处

电话: 0755-5590159

传真: 5590160

进藏外交官与外国记者等由区外事办公室接待并负责办理进藏确认函。

进藏工作、进行商贸活动的外国人由外经贸厅接待并负责办理进藏确认函。

进藏探亲的外籍藏胞，由统战部接待、负责办理进藏确认函。

飞 机

可乘北京至拉萨、成都至拉萨、西安至拉萨、重庆至拉萨、广州至拉萨、上海至拉萨、昆明至拉萨、香港至拉萨航班。成都至拉萨航班最多，每天都有两班往返。乘飞机单程时间不到2小时。拉萨贡嘎机场距市区97公里，乘车一小时左右即可抵达。途径雅鲁藏布江最长的曲水大桥，并可观赏沿途山水和田园风光，也可沿途停车游览卓玛拉康。

长途汽车

可在格尔木、西宁、成都乘坐带有旅游标志的客车到拉萨，正常行程1至5天，夏天需带毛衣，冬天需穿羽绒衣。

中巴车

拉萨的中巴车分8条线路从市中心向市郊辐射。招手即停，十分便捷。

出租汽车

拉萨出租汽车穿梭如云，在市区内不计程，昼夜一律10元。去远郊可与司机议价。

三轮车

人力三轮车是辅助的交通工具。短距离路程、携带行李或前往汽车不便驶入的小巷，坐三轮车更为方便。

自行车

拉萨人上下班或外出，多以自行车为代步工具。市区道路平坦，许多道路设有自行车专用道路，与机动车之间以绿化带隔离，窄的街面上划有分道线。涉外宾馆、旅店备有出租自行车供外宾租用。

邮政局

邮电局是西藏自治区邮政通信中心，主要经营信函、包裹、汇兑、储蓄、报刊发行等业务。目前，对国内近二百个大中城市开通了邮政快件、特快传递、集邮、电报、电话业务。

地址：拉萨市北京东路64号

电信局

电信局是西藏高原通信区的电信枢纽局兰西拉光缆线路

的终端。目前，已开通的项目有：各类电报、市内电话、人工直拨长途电话、移动电话、磁卡电话、电话会议，会议电视、１２６数字寻呼、１２７全国自动联网寻呼、１２８中文寻呼、１６６语音电子信箱、１６８电话信息服务、１１２障碍自动管理、１１４自动查号等。

地址：拉萨市林廓东路59号

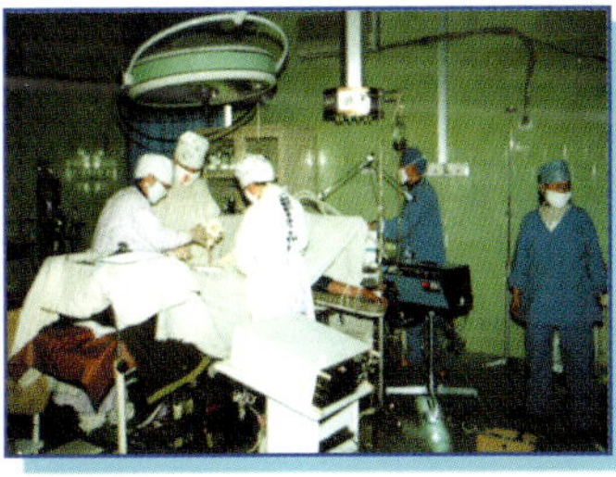

医疗服务机构

拉萨的医疗服务机构非常多，大的有区属、市属医院，小的有各门诊服务点。需要时可与本书推荐的医院联系。

西藏自治区人民医院

地址：拉萨市林廓北路

电话：6332462

西藏自治区第二人民医院

地址：金珠东路8号

电话：6324883

西藏自治区藏医院

地址：娘热路14号

电话：6323428

西藏军区总医院

地址：娘热路北路

电话:6323390

拉萨市人民医院

地址：北京东路

电话:6323212

6323338

高原保健常识

拉萨海拔高、气压低、空气密度小，平均含氧量６８％。日照长、光照强，冬季漫长寒冷而无盛夏。年降雨量少，冬、春季尤为干燥。高原气候垂直变化显著，昼夜温差大。大多数人初到高原，不同程度有高原反应。如：头痛、呼吸急促、恶心、呕吐、失眠等症状。这时切忌剧烈活动，衣着要适当，避免感冒。一般过2－3天后，症状会逐步减轻或消失。但有严重心脏病、肺病、高血压者不宜到高原旅游。进藏时间选在4－10月最适宜。进藏前身体要调整到良好状态，不要带病进藏。乘飞机前睡眠要充足，下机后动作应缓慢。避免提重物，可多做深

呼吸。必要时可根据医嘱服药，如：镇静剂、氨茶碱等。含服或泡服人参对缓解高原反应有一定的效果。如感极端缺氧，可及时吸氧（宾馆、饭店、医院等可提供）。若患感冒等疾病，要及时治疗，以免恶化成肺气肿等。外出最好戴上墨镜或防晒帽，擦防晒霜，以防止紫外线灼伤皮肤。初到高原进食莫过量，可多吃些蔬菜、水果。多喝水，尽量少吸烟，少喝酒。

衣 着

拉萨的气候特点是早晚温差大。旅游者春秋到拉萨时须穿毛衣毛裤。冬季白天温度较暖，但早晚寒冷，须携带羽绒服或棉大衣。

拉萨市气温表

TEMPERATURE

月份	1	2	3	4	5	6	7	8	9	10	11	12
Month	Jan	Feb	Mar	Apr	May	Jun	Jul	Aug	Sep	Oct	Nov	Dec
最高 Highest	6.8	9.2	12.0	15.7	19.7	22.5	21.7	20.7	19.6	16.4	11.6	7.7
最低 Lowest	-10.2	-6.9	-3.2	0.9	5.1	9.2	9.9	9.4	7.6	1.4	-5.0	-9.1
平均 Average	-2.3	1.1	4.5	8.3	12.3	15.4	15.1	14.3	12.7	8.2	2.3	-1.7

民航航班

国际航班:

加德满都-拉萨　SZ407/SZ408　周二　周四　周六

国内航班:

香港-拉萨　(包机)

北京-拉萨　SZ4111　每天

昆明-拉萨　SZ4429　周一

上海-拉萨　SZ4812　周三　周日

广州-拉萨　SZ4312　周一

成都-拉萨　SZ4402/SZ4404/SZ4111　每天

重庆-拉萨　SZS4311　周一

西安-拉萨　SZ4811/SZ4218　周一　周三　周五　周日

长途客运路线:

自治区内:

拉萨-山南　每日3班

拉萨-林芝　每日1班

拉萨-日喀则　每日3班

拉萨-那曲　每日3班

拉萨-昌都　每月3班

(5号、15号、25号发车)

自治区外:

拉萨一成都　每日2班

拉萨一重庆　每日1班

拉萨一格尔木　每日1班

拉萨一西宁　每日1班

拉萨一兰州　每日1班

观光游览 TOUR AND SIGHTSEEING

雪域古城拉萨，这个中国西南边陲的重要城市，是西藏政治、经济、文化、宗教中心和交通枢纽，是藏传佛教圣地，是中国重要历史文化名城之一。并已被联合国教科文组织列入《世界文化遗产名录》。素以历史悠久、文化灿烂、风土人情独特、名胜古迹众多、宗教色彩浓厚而闻名世界。拉萨共有名胜古迹、佛教圣地及景点２００多处。已开发的景点２０多处，还有３０多处正在开发。不仅

有闻名于世的布达拉宫，黄教三大寺、大昭寺、小昭寺、罗布林卡，还有众多的古建筑、墓

葬、石窟、摹崖造像、金石匾额、库存文物以及古遗址等。还有神奇的纳木错高原湖泊风光，美丽的当雄草原风光，神奇的德仲温泉和林园、墨竹工卡等自然保护区。

拉萨以其独特的地理位置，瑰丽的自然风光，丰富的自然资源，悠久的历史，灿烂的民族文化，别具一格的风俗习惯，不胜枚举的文化古迹，独一无二的佛教色彩吸引着国内外越来越多的旅游观光者、登山探险者、科学考察人员。

拉萨各族人民热诚欢迎海内外各界宾朋前来观光旅游。

寺院 PLACES OF WORSHIP

布达拉宫

位于拉萨市中心，是世界文化遗产，国家重点文物保护单位。初建于7世纪松赞干布时期，距今已有一千三百多年的历史。是西藏现存最大最完整的古堡建筑群，是历代达赖喇嘛生活起居和进行政治活动的场所，也是西藏政教合一统治权力的中心。

布达拉宫是地球上海拔最高的古代宫堡。它集中了藏汉民族建筑艺术的精华，矗立在古城拉萨红山之巅。高177.19米，海拔３７００多米，东西长３６０余米，南北宽２７０米，占地面积３６万余平方米。

布达拉宫由红宫、白宫两大部分组成，红宫居中、白宫横贯两翼，红白相间，群楼重叠，是集宫殿、城堡和寺院于一体的宏伟建筑。

大昭寺

大昭寺，是国务院公布的全国文物保护单位。是西藏驰名中外的最大的古寺庙。该寺是纪念松赞干布迎娶唐朝文成公主，尼泊尔尺尊公主而兴。建于七世纪中叶。十多个世纪以来，经历代多次修葺和改扩建，形成今天占地２５１００平方米的宏大建筑群。整个建筑风格独特，雄奇壮观，金碧辉煌的鎏金宝顶，丹垩相映的高墙和富丽堂皇的装饰，组成仙境琼阁的朝拜圣地。大昭寺的主殿有三层，加上四角的神殿，共四层，以释迦牟尼殿为主的２０多个佛殿里，摆满了大小不等的金、铜及泥塑像。上中下三层的回廊都绘有各种题材的壁画。这些高超的建筑工艺，不仅体现了藏族人民的勤劳与智慧，也是藏汉两兄弟民族友好相处的历史见证。

哲蚌寺

哲蚌寺坐落在拉萨市西郊约10公里外的根碚乌孜山南坡的山坳里。规模宏大，远观殿宇鳞次栉比，铺满山坡。入内行道纵横，犹如一座小镇。该寺系宗喀巴的著名弟子绎央曲杰·扎西具丹于公元1416年创建的，为黄教三大寺之一。

哲蚌寺主要由措钦大殿、四大扎仓和甘丹颇章几部分组成，总建筑面积25万平方米，在大殿和经堂的外部采用金顶、相轮、宝幢、八宝等佛教题材的饰物加以装饰，增强了佛教庄严气氛，被建筑烘托得更加富丽堂皇。哲蚌寺是世界最大的寺院，其建筑规模和在寺喇嘛人数为世界之最。

色拉寺

色拉寺，位于拉萨北郊约4公里处的色拉乌孜山南麓，占地面积11.5万平方米，是黄教三大寺之一。该寺是黄教大师宗喀巴的弟子释迦耶歇

主持修建的，建于公元1419年，由措钦大殿、3个扎仓、30个康村组成。措钦大殿顶层，装饰歇山式金顶，屋脊上装饰宝盘、宝珠、倒幢、人身神鸟、四个翅角饰摩羯鱼首，金顶下采用内地的斗拱形成飞檐，更增加了大殿的宗教气氛。

甘丹寺

甘丹寺，位于拉萨市达孜县河南岸的旺古尔山坳里。是黄教三大寺之一，全国重点文物保护单位。

小昭寺

小昭寺，地处拉萨市市中心，位于大昭寺北约500米处。始建于公元647年，与大昭寺同时完工。该寺坐西朝东，占地约4000平方米。其前部是个庭院，后部是神殿门楼、转经回廊等附属建筑。小昭寺是一座深受藏族人民敬仰的古寺。

罗布林卡

罗布林卡，位于拉萨城西。1988年，被列为全国重点文物保护单位。

清乾隆二十年（1755年）七世达赖格桑加措在此修建格桑颇章宫殿，作为夏季休憩之所。每年藏历四月至九月达赖在此处理政务，举行各种庆典。以后成为历世达赖的夏宫。

罗布林卡像一座博物馆，向人们展示了西藏各个时期历史、文化、艺术多姿多彩的风貌。

热振寺

热振寺，是西藏自治区重点文物保护单位之一，位于拉萨东北部的林周县汤果乡。是西藏最早建成的寺庙之一。北宋嘉祐元年（1056年）由藏传佛教噶当派创始人仲敦巴建立，是噶当派第一寺院。

热振寺背靠崖山，清泉淙淙，翠柏葱郁，红墙碧瓦掩映其间，幽谷氤氲，峰峦吐秀。身临其境，顿觉心旷神怡。佛地宝刹，名不虚传。

楚布寺

楚布寺，位于拉萨以西堆龙德庆县境内。寺后有白玛琼宗山，林木葱郁，岩壁上有"能人大佛"的自生形象，挺胸凸肚，端坐兀立，东山白云飘拂，西山形如白度母亭亭玉立。噶玛巴堆松钦巴于公元1159年来到这里，见幽雅宜人，于是长住修行。后出游康地，寿高八十岁时才返回堆龙并兴建楚布寺。寺内保存明代以来文物甚多。

琉璃桥

琉璃桥，位于大昭寺西约300米处，宇拓路东头以南，原是连接拉萨古城内外的要道之一。琉璃桥为石筑，五孔梁桥，跨度28.3米，桥面宽6.8米。桥上东西两侧砌有石墙，墙厚1.6米，高3.2米。西边墙顶端托人字形屋顶，覆绿色琉璃瓦四角为龙首正檐，屋脊中饰一米高的琉璃宝瓶，两端有琉璃供果脊饰。这座漂亮耀眼的歇山式桥梁是藏汉古建筑之一。

唐蕃会盟碑

此碑，又称甥舅和盟碑、

长庆会盟碑。位于大昭寺正门前公主柳旁。碑身高4.78米，宽0.50米，顶端有石帽覆盖，帽上有顶，基角为石龟背负状。

公元822年唐廷遣使会盟于吐蕃首府拉萨，不仅先后会盟立誓，还于公元823年在拉萨将盟誓刻于碑石上，立于大昭寺前。此碑不仅体现了藏汉民族的希望和心愿，而且是藏汉民族友谊长存的重要历史见证。

外 碑

外碑，藏语称“多仁玛”。位于布达拉宫前院墙大门外，与布达拉宫山脚石阶下的一座无字碑相对，古称之为“外碑”。

碑上有石顶石帽覆盖，碑身三面刻有藏文，一面空白。此碑是藏区内迄今所见最早的一座。赤松德赞时期，赞普为表彰他的内臣达扎路恭的功绩而亲颂盟誓诏文，且明令勒碑。

羊八井地热区

拉萨地热资源丰富，最著名的应属羊八井地热蒸气田。它位于当雄县境内，方圆7000多平方米，温度保持在47℃左右，是中国大陆上开发的第一个湿蒸气田。是世界上海拔最高的地热发电站。地热田的东北部有一个面积7350平方米深达16米的热水湖，水湛蓝，热水不断地从下往上翻滚，湖面水温在47-59℃之间，湖边建有浴室，人们可以在这里洗上一个舒适的温泉澡。

融融热流的羊八井蒸气田在白雪皑皑的群山怀抱之中，这一完美的契合，构成了世界屋脊上引人入胜的天然奇观。

德仲温泉

位于墨竹工卡县门巴区德仲乡，海拔4300多米。温泉的温度为42℃，流量为68升/秒。该温泉具有许多特殊疗效，被专家称为“世界第一温泉”。

纳木错

位于拉萨市当雄县境内。纳木错，藏语意为“天湖”，是人们心目中的神湖。每年吸引着众多的信徒不远万里来此朝圣，以寻求一次灵魂上的超越。

纳木错，湖水清澈，成群的细鳞鱼和无鳞鱼在湖里游来游去。夏季，成群的野鸭、鱼鸥、和鹭鸶飞舞在湖边的浅滩和湖中的岩岛上。湖滨地区水草丰美，常有野牦牛、黄羊、狼、狐狸和兔子出没。湛蓝的湖水和雪白的山峰相映成趣，构成了西藏最美丽的自然景观 。

八廓街

是围绕大昭寺修建的一条拉萨最繁华的商业街，大都销售当地和印度、尼泊尔生产的具有浓郁民族特色的轻工业产品和手工艺品，这里也是藏族佛教徒转经的最重要的线路。

布达拉宫广场

位于拉萨市中心，是自治区举行重大集会的地方。1995年，西藏自治区三十周年大庆典礼在此举行。此活动为广场建成后的首次使用。2001年，西藏自治区和平解放50周年大庆典礼也在这里隆重举行。

广场的正前方是依山叠砌，殿宇巍峨，气势雄伟的布达拉宫。广场的中心建有大型喷泉莲花池，具有浓郁的民族色彩。

每逢节日，这里都举行隆重的升旗仪式。整个广场花灯如昼、喷泉似锦、人潮如流，是市民和旅客最喜欢的地方之一。

宗角禄康公园

人工圣湖龙王潭，龙王潭是拉萨著名的园林，位于宗角禄康公园内，是公元17世纪五世达赖重建布达拉宫时掘土形成的人工湖。后来，六世达赖在湖心的小山上建了一幢三层楼阁，命名为“龙宫”，龙王潭由此得名。

拉萨市旅游景点示意图
Lhasa Scenic Spots

Traditions and Customs 民俗风情

拉萨是以藏族为主的少数民族地区。藏族有自己的语言文字。藏族人普遍信仰佛教。宗教作为文化现象已渗透到拉萨社会的各个领域，并对人们的生产、日常生活、娱乐产生广泛而深刻的影响。藏族无姓，名字一般为四个字或两个字，多限于吉祥用语。藏族人性格豪放，能歌善舞。藏族以丰富多彩的传统的娱乐活动、独特的服饰、饮食、民居、婚丧等文化习俗构成了独具特色的人文景观。

语言

拉萨的藏族一般讲藏语，但绝大多数的藏族群众都会讲一口流利的普通话。凡是涉外宾馆、饭店、旅馆、餐厅、商店都有汉、藏、英文字标牌，配备英语翻译。但是在街上不易碰到懂外语的人。外出游览最好是团队集体出行，有翻译陪同。国内旅客来拉萨，尽管大胆外出，拉萨民风淳朴，群众很乐于为人指路。

衣、食、住

衣：藏族传统服饰袖长、腰宽、襟大的特点。常在领、袖、襟和下摆连沿镶花色布料或绸子。农区多以氆氇、毛料、呢子和布为原料。女士衣裙

一般无袖，装束时需配一色彩鲜艳的衬衣和围裙。而牧区多以皮类材质为主，较肥大。

食：藏族传统食物和饮料有糌粑、面粉、风干肉、手抓牛羊肉、奶制品、酥油茶、甜茶和青稞酒等。

住：农区藏式民居多为石

木结构式平顶房，一般是二至三层，回廊内院形式，屋内摆设精雕细制的藏式家具与各种装饰。而牧区多以帐篷为主，质料有布料和毛皮之分。

民俗节日

除国家法定的节日外，藏族还有许多传统的民族节日，独具民族风情。

藏历年

藏历元月一日

藏族原来没有年历，把桃花开的日子作为一年的开始。现在的藏历起源于公元1027年。从那时起，藏历的第一天，便定为藏历年。藏历年是西藏最大的节日，节日期间，人们准备年货，家家户户团聚，互道"扎西德勒"，载歌载舞欢庆节日。

传召大法会

藏历元月初四至二十四日

西藏最大的宗教节日，此会是由格鲁派创始人宗喀巴于1409年在拉萨发起的一次祈祷大法会延续而来的。期间西藏三大寺的僧人近2万人集中在大昭寺向释迦牟尼的佛像祈祷，并举行格西学位的考试。西藏其他地方的佛教信徒也来此朝佛，发放布施。

酥油花灯节

藏历元月十五日

传召大法会的最后一天是为庆祝释迦牟尼与其他教派辩论获胜的日子。人们在大昭寺和八廓街上陈列酥油花、酥油灯，通宵达旦地歌舞庆贺。当夜幕降临，街道的花架上五颜六色的酥油灯点燃后，一片辉煌。花灯上有五彩油塑的花卉，还有惟妙惟肖的各种人物和飞禽走兽。用酥油制作的多姿多彩的酥油花盘，做工精巧，色泽绚丽，形象逼真。每到这一天，拉萨便成了欢乐的海洋。

萨噶达瓦节

藏历 4 月

相传藏历4月15日是释迦牟尼诞生、成佛、圆寂的日子。每年这一天，信徒便围绕着布达拉宫和大昭寺转经进行祈祷，对释迦牟尼的金像进行顶礼膜拜；为龙王潭的神龙像添灯祭供，祈祷风调雨顺、五谷丰登。然后，人们聚集在龙王潭划船、歌舞、逛林卡。整个藏历 4 月，僧俗群众不吃肉、不杀生，专心转经朝佛。

当雄赛马节

藏历 7 月

赛马射箭是藏族人民传统竞赛活动之一。以前赛马仅限于赛马、射箭和骑马射箭三项，而今的赛马节不仅增加了其他的文化活动，还成了物资交流的一个盛会。赛马节已成为拉萨地区最盛大的地区性节日。

朝山节

藏历六月一日至七月十五日

佛教信徒认为这一天是释迦牟尼第一次举行讲经的日子。这天人们穿着新衣，带着食品，赶往拉藏附近山上各寺朝佛、念经。之后，到野外尽情狂欢，直到日落才返回城里。

雪顿节

藏历六月底至七月中旬

西藏最大的节日之一。雪顿节藏语意为“吃酸奶子的节日”。后来由于雪顿节的活动内容逐渐演变为以藏戏会演为聚在罗布林卡连续几天进行表演和比赛。此外，还开展各种物资交流会。

沐浴节

藏历七月六日至十二日

传说天上有一颗叫“弃山”的星出现时，若能到河边洗澡，将有益于身体健康。因此每年的七月，当“弃山”星出现的一个星期中，人们来到河边进行圣洁的沐浴，以求平安、健康。

望果节

藏历八月

是西藏人民渴望丰收的节日，于秋收前择日举行，历时1至3天。届时，人们用哈达缠着青稞、麦穗做成的丰收塔，敲锣打鼓，唱着颂歌，绕地头转圈，然后进行骑马比赛。节日一过便开始秋收。

燃灯节

藏历十月

传说，这天是宗喀巴的圆寂日，所以家家户户在房顶上点燃无数的酥油灯念经歌颂宗喀巴，以示纪念。

驱鬼节

藏历十二月二十九日

每年藏历十二月二十九日，布达拉宫就要举行一次盛大的跳神活动，各寺庙也举行类似的活动。以此为新的一年驱鬼消灾。

民族手工业

拉萨的民族手工业有着悠久的历史。工艺品种类繁多，色彩斑斓是中华民族艺术宝库中的一颗瑰丽的明珠。其中，有具有鲜明民族特色的氆氇、地毯、围裙、藏腰刀，还有藏被、藏装、藏靴、藏帽、藏垫、木碗、陶器，以及金属加工的装饰品等。

拉萨的民族手工业，为加深各国之间的友谊，增强各族人民的了解，架起了金色的桥梁。

购物

拉萨市商业网点不断增加，通常大家会去以下商场购物（营业时间为9：30－20：00）。

八廓街市场

地址：八廓街内

主要经营：民族手工艺品、宗教旅游产品、民族服装、鞋帽等。

国贸大厦

地址：宇拓路

主要经营：副食、日用百货、五金交电、服装、文体用品等。

金谷商场

地址：宇拓路

主要经营：日用百货、服装、鞋业、家电、副食品等。

拉萨百货大楼

地址：宇拓路

主要经营：日用百货、家电、食品、针纺织品、文体用品、化妆品、民族手工艺品。

青年路市场

这里是服装一条街

除以上购物场所外，拉萨还有很多不同形式的贸易机构，旅游消费者随意前往参观购物。

拉萨商业宾馆

拉萨商业宾馆位于拉萨市中心康昂东路，紧邻世界著名的布达拉宫，与西藏自治区政府隔街相望，交通、通迅、购物及办公都十分便捷。

宾馆拥有标准间、豪华套房47间（套），硬件已达到涉外三星级标准，全天24小时供应热水。大厅设有西式小咖啡厅供宾客休息。商务中心、美容美发厅、茶园和大小会议室一应俱全，并可根据宾客要求代办旅游接待、机票订购服务。宽敞明亮的各式餐厅，除了为您提供美味的藏汉佳肴，还可承接大小晚宴会及各种庆典活动。

“宾客至上，服务第一”是我们的宗旨，热忱欢迎各界朋友的光临惠顾。

Lhasa Commercial Hotel

Lhasa Commercial Hotel is located in east Kang Ang Road, centerof Lhasa, neibouring the world famous Potala Palace and Tibet autonomous government, enjoying convenient transportation, communication, ideal for shopping and working.

The hotel has 47 standard guestrooms and suites with 24-hour hot water supplying. There is a west-styled coffee shop in the lobby, while business center, beauty salon, tea house and meeting rooms of different sizes are all available, offering services such as travel, ticket booking, ect. The spacious and bright restaurants provide wonderful cuisine of both Han and Tibet styles, ideal for banquets and celebrations.

地址：康昂东路8号

电话：6325888

北京加州肥牛酒楼 Beijing California Beef Hot Pot Restaurant

北京加州肥牛酒楼是一家风味独特的酒楼，地处拉萨市民族北路，距布达拉宫、罗布林卡等旅游胜地只有1至2公里路程。

酒楼主营肥牛火锅、新派川味中餐及风味小吃，可同时容纳200—250人就餐。一层零点，二、三层共有大小包间12间，三层包间还备有卡拉OK音响、室内空调等设备，是朋友聚会，团队用餐，喜庆婚宴的良好场所。

地址：西藏自治区拉萨市民族北路
电话：0891－6830300
传真：0891－6830226

Beijing California Beef Hot Pot Restaurant is a special flavor restaurant, located in Minzu North Road, Lhasa, only 1-2 km from Potala Palace and Norbu Lingka.

It features beef hot pot, new-styled Sichuan cuisine and local snacks, able to accommodate 200 up to 250 diners. It provides a la carte menu on the first floor, while the 12 private rooms are on the second floor and the third floor with karaoke and air-conditioning.

The restaurant is an ideal place for gathering, group dinner, as well as wedding party

Tel：0891－6830300
Fax：0891－6830226

西藏拉萨高原旅馆

LHASA HLGHLAND HOTEL

法人代表：洛旦

Legal person:Lao Dan

高原旅馆地址：拉萨市纳金路74号

Add(Highland Hotel) :74, Najin Road, Lhasa

电话：（0891）6324916　6326084

Tel:(0891)6324916　6326084

高原旅馆拥有不同等级的客房和经济间68间，设248个床位。旅馆还设有拉萨地区一流的停车场，可一次性停放100多辆车，停车场内设有修理部，随时为旅客提供方便。

高原宾馆现有客房36间，88个床位。客房部局合理，从标准间到普通客房、规格齐全、价格合理，可以满足各层次旅客的要求，宾馆24小时供应热、开水，可停放40多辆车。

高原旅馆、高原宾馆地处繁华地段，到布达拉宫、大昭寺、八廓街只需十几分钟，代办长途汽车、预定机票、国际国内直拨电话业务，并设有民族风味餐厅等服务项目。

我们的服务宗旨是“旅客至上、信誉第一”，以文明优质的服务取得旅客的信赖。高原旅馆、高原宾馆以优质热情的服务欢迎您的光临！

Lhasa Highland Hotel and Lhasa Plateau Guest House are ideally located and provide services such as ticket-booking, IDD, DDD as well as cuisine of national flavor.

Lhasa Highland Hotel and Plateau Guest House are all foreign-oriented hotels. Highlahd hotel has 68 guest rooms with 248 beds. It has a first-rate garage in which can park 100 automobiles.

Lhasa Plateau Guest House has 36 guest houses with 88 beds offering 24-hour hot water. It is ideal for tourists to stay.

西藏拉萨高原宾馆

LHASA PLATEAU GUESTHOUSE

电话：(0891)6327814　6327791

Tel：(0891)6327814　6327791

邮编：850000

p.c:850000

高原宾馆地址：拉萨市当热路

Add(Plateau Guest House):Daura Road, Lhasa

敦固宾馆

DHOOD GU HOTEL

地址：拉萨市北京中路冲塞康夏萨苏路1

敦固宾馆是由中外合资，拉萨敦固宾馆有限责任公司投资兴建的一家具有三星级标准的涉外旅游宾馆。

它位于拉萨市中心—冲赛康夏萨苏黄金路段，交通极为便利。宾馆朝南100米即为大昭寺，朝北300米即为小昭寺，这些都是著名的观光景点。

敦固宾馆采用纯藏族风格，客房内设施齐全，配有中央空调、卫星电视、IDD等现代化设备，并24小时供应冷、热水。

敦固宾馆同时还有藏式餐厅、西式餐厅、咖啡屋、顶层酒吧、西点面包、商务中心和电子邮件服务。敦固宾馆以其藏式特色，优良的环境和完善的服务及设施使您达到满意。

敦固宾馆的全体员工恭候您的光临！

ADD: 19#Shasarsu road, Trom Si Khang, Lhas
TEL: 0891-6322555 6346910
FAX: 0891-6323555

Dhood Gu Hotel is a joint venture hotel. Dhood Gu Hotel is located at Shasarsu Road, Trom Si Khang which is the center of Lhasa city. The traffic is convenient for travellers and businessmen. On the south, it is 100 meters from Jokhang and on the north, it is 300 meters from Ramoche. They are all famous scenic spots.

Dhood Gu Hotel is fully decorated in typical Tibetan styles and equipped with first rate facilities in all rooms such as air-conditioners, satellite TV, IDD, 24-hour hot water service.

The Dhood Gu Hotel also offers a wide rang of services and extensive facilities such as Tibetan restaurant, western restaurant, coffee shop, roof-top bar, business center, bakery shop, and E-mail service.

The Dhood Gu Hotel will make you feel satisfied with the best environment , perfect facilities and excellent serves.

琅赛宾馆

Langsai Hotel

琅赛宾馆坐落在闻名世界的日光城拉萨，位于布达拉宫与色拉寺之间的拉萨当热东路。宾馆环境幽雅，设施完备，交通便利，是您来藏观光旅游及洽谈业务的理想的下榻之处。

琅赛宾馆是按二星级酒店标准设计建造的具有民族建筑风格和现代功能相结合的涉外宾馆。她拥有宽敞、舒适的各类客房能够满足不同经济层的需求，并提供藏、中餐为主的风味餐饮服务。优势的地理环境，设备齐全的桑拿中心以及装饰较好的多功能厅和商务中心，加之训练有素的员工队伍，24小时的保安值勤和热水供应服务以及风格独特的藏汉式会议室，将给您进行商谈和各种会议提供舒适和方便.

琅赛宾馆全体员工恭候您的光临，祝您永远扎西德勒！

Located in the world famous sunlight city Lhasa, standing on the Daura East Road between Potala Palace and Sera Monastery, Langsai Hotel is well equipped, enjoying an elegant environment and convenient communication, ideal both for businessmen and travellers.

It is a foreign-oriented hotel constructed under the two-star level, integrating strong national architect style with modern functions. It boasts spacious and comfortable suite, standard rooms and economical rooms, able to meet different levels of demands, providing food and services.

The well-equipped sauna center, finely-appointed function room and business center, 24-hour safe guard and hot water supplying, together with well-trained staff and special-styled conference room, bring you great convenience and comfort for negotiation and meeting. You will find complete function and high quality service in the Langsai Hotel.

We are awaiting you respectfully and wishing you ZHAXIDELE!

新世

新世纪宾馆是一家三星级标准涉外定点宾馆，地处拉萨市中心繁华地段，拥有客房80间（套），均配有冰箱及小酒吧等。推开客房窗户即见布达拉宫，饭后漫步即达大昭寺和八角街，西郊罗布林卡，交通便利，自设超市、商场，登临茶楼鸟瞰全市。饭店软、硬件达标，管理严谨、服务一流，是您来藏商务、旅游的理想之地，是您温馨的高原之家。

愿热情、纯朴的新世纪人为您的选择留下美好回忆，愿相聚的缘和扎西德勒伴您一生走。

New Century Hotel

纪宾馆

New Century Hotel is a three-star level, foreign-oriented hotel, situated in the prosperous area in the center of Lhasa, boasting 80 guest rooms and suites equipped with refrigerator and mini-bar. Outside the room window is Potala Palace, and the Jokhang Monastery, Bajiao Street and Norbu Lingka are within walking distance, supermarket and shopping arcade are also available. Stepping up to the teahouse, you can enjoy a bird view over the whole city.

With comprehensive functions, efficient management and first class service, the hotel is the warm home on the plateau, ideal both for businessmen and travellers.

We hope the enthusiastic and rustic staff of the hotel will give you a wonderful impression, and wish you ZHAXIDELE!

西藏天河宾馆简介

Tibet Tianhe Hotel

西藏天河宾馆是西藏定点涉外旅游宾馆。位于拉萨市宇拓路，地处市中心，是商业旅游黄金地段，交通便捷；东邻拉萨古城八廓街及大昭寺，西依宏伟壮观的布达拉宫，步行5分钟就可到达上述景点。

宾馆设施先进、齐全，集客房、餐饮、休闲、娱乐、商务为一体，已达到三星级标准。“信誉第一，服务第一，质量第一”是我们的服务宗旨，西藏天河宾馆将以安全、舒适、温馨的环境，完善的设施为您提供尽善尽美的服务。

西藏天河宾馆随时欢迎您的光临！

地址：拉萨市宇拓路5号

Tibet Tianhe Hotel is a designated tourist hotel. It is located at Yutok Road, Lhasa, the golden place of commerce and tourism with convenient transportation.

"Prestige first, service first and quality first" is our business aim.

Tibet Tianhe Hotel will provide you with best services offering safe, comfortable and enjoyable environment and consummate facilities.

Welcome to Tibet Tianhe Hotel.

ADD: 5, Yutuo Road, Lhasa
TEL: 0891-6338138
FAX: 0891-6339562

西藏虹桥宾馆

TIBET HONG QIAO HOTEL

虹桥宾馆位于高原古城拉萨市中心，距闻名世界的布达拉宫、大昭寺仅咫尺之遥。地理位置适中，交通便利，是您商业活动、观光旅游的最佳选择。

崭新的虹桥宾馆，功能齐备、服务一流。下榻虹桥宾馆，使您有如宾至如归。

宾馆拥有汉、藏式宴会厅8个。全面提供上乘川菜、粤菜、藏式菜肴。

虹桥宾馆全体员工竭诚为您服务，让您尽享雪域高原的热情。

地址：拉萨市北京东路161号

ADD: 161,Beijing Dong Road, Lhasa

TEL: 0891-6320088

FAX: 0891-6345174

Tibet Hong Qiao Hotel is located in the center of ancient Lhasa city. It's very close to the famouse Potala Palace. Jokhang Temple. A great convenience for the traffic. An ideal place for commercial business and travel.

New Tibet Hong Qiao Hotel is equipped and provided with excellent service. You will feel at home in the hotel.

There are 60 rooms and suites with closed-TV. IDD&DDD.

There are 8 kind of banquet hall with Han and Tibetan style. You can enjoy all kind of beautiful cuisine in Hong Qiao Hotel, Sichuan. Cantonese and Tibetan style food will offer for you.

You are always welcome in Hong Qiao Hotel.

西藏天域交通宾馆 Tibet Tianyu Communication Hotel

西藏天域交通宾馆

西域天域交通宾馆是按三星级标准设计建造的涉外酒店，离世界著名的布达拉宫仅300米，距罗布林卡、中国银行仅200米。

新装登场的西藏天域交通宾馆功能完善，服务细微，能给您居家的感受。

宾馆拥有客房112间，分为标准间、贵宾房、豪华套房、藏式套房，房间装有空调、闭路电视、国际国内长途、饮水机。宾馆拥有能同时提供300人就餐的餐厅，为您提供川菜、粤菜和藏式菜肴，让您享受美食的乐趣。

宾至如归、服务至上是我们的服务宗旨。

总经理：王先华
副总经理：张成
销售部联系人：唐瑜苹
电话：0891-6832166-8588
手机：13908989856

Constructed under the three-star level, Tibet Tianyu Communication Hotel is an foreign-oriented hotel, 300 meters away from the world famous Potala Palace and 200 meters away from the Norbu Lingka or and Bank of China .

The newly-opened hotel is of complete function and considerate service, which make you feel at home.

It has 112 guest rooms, including standard rooms, VIP rooms, deluxe suites and Tibetan-styled suites, all equipped with air-conditioning, in-house movie, IDD, DDD and water machine. The restaurants in the hotel provide Sichuan, Contonese, and Tibet style cuisines, able to accomodate up to 300 diners, enabling you to enjoy the delicious food here.

'Home away from home' is the service principle of our hotel.

General Manager: Wang Xianhua
Vice General Manager: Zhang Cheng
Sales Department Person in Charge: Tang Yuping
Tel: (0891)6832166 ext.8588
Mobile Phone: 13908989856

Facts Of Lhasa

FACTS ON LHASA

Lhasa is the capital city of Tibet Autonomous Region. It is also the political, economic and cultural center of Tibet as well as the communication hub. As the holy land of Tibetan Sect of Buddism, Lhasa enjoys a long history. It is one of the famous historical and cultural cities of the world and an ancient city that is full of vitality and marching towards modernization.

GEOGRAPHICAL LOCATION

Lhasa is situated in the valley plain at the north bank of Lhasa River, which is the tributary of Yarlungzangbo River. The location of Lhasa is 91' 6" east longitude and 29' 6" north latitude. The span of it is 277KM. Surrounded by 4 prefectures and 11 Counties, Lhasa represents a large city on the plateau to the southwest border of our country.

TERRAIN AND LANDFORMS

The vast land of Lhasa with complicated landforms covers and area of 29,539 square kilometers, of which 544 square kilometers are urban area. The average altitude is 3658 meters. The northern most

part of the city, elevated at 4200-4900 meters above sea level, is a joint belt with rising hills and many natural grasslands between southern part and northern part of Tibet. The biggest salt water lake, Nam Co lake is inside the boundary of Lhasa. Mountain Nianqing Tanggula is located to the northwest of the city and to the east of Mountain Himalaya. It is more than 5000 meters above sea level with a pleasant climate.

NATURAL RESOURCES

The natural condition of Lhasa is unique. The complexity of landforms and varied natural conditions have gifted Lhasa with many rich natural resources. Rivers that run lengthwise and crosswise through the 29,539 square kilometers land create great hydraulic potentials. The endless snow mountain valley and plateau are endowed with rich mineral resources. The vast grassland at Damxung, unique underground heat resources and hot springs, fertile river valley plain and many varieties of animals and plants have all made Lhasa a piece of beautiful land on the plateau.

CLIMATE

Lhasa is surrounded by mountains and rivers with a comfortable climate. The highest temperature of the year is 28 degrees Celsius and the lowest is minus 14, and the annual average temperature is 8 degrees. Rainfall comes mainly in July, August and September and the annual rainfall is 500 millimeters. The sunshine hours of Lhasa are over 3,000 annually, so it is nicknamed the "City of Sunlight", which has made it a rare summer resort.

HISTORY

Lhasa means "Sacred Land" in Tibetan language. The history can be traced back to 1,300 years ago. As early as the 7th century, after King Songtsan Gambo united Tibet, he moved the capital to Resa (now Lhasa). At that time, this place was still a piece of desolate and inhabited land. King Songtsan Gambo built palaces (the original Potala Palace) on Jiangshan mountain. Subsequently, Jokhang Monastery and Ramoche Monastery were constructed and an ancient city came into being. Lhasa was liberated peacefully in 1951 and approved as a city in 1960. Now, 7 counties and 1 district, which are Dolongdeqen, Damxung, Nyemo, Quxur, Dagze, Maizhokunggar, Lhunzhub Counties and Chengguan District, are under its municipal administration.

PEOPLE AND NATIONALITIES

Lhasa has a population of 480,000, about 200,000 of which live in the urban area. There are 31 nationalities in this region, including Tibetans, Hans and Huis. Tibetan people account for 89.7% of the population.

SCIENCE AND TECHNOLOGY

The scientific and technological works of Lhasa started in the 1970's. The past 30 years have seen the establishment of nearly 20 scientific and technological research institutions. More than 6,000 science and technology workers at all levels promoted the development of science and technology of the city.

EDUCATION

Before liberation, there was not even a real school in Lhasa. In the 50 years after the peaceful liberation of Tibet, the educational undertaking has grown to a certain scale out of nothing and developed in a coordinated stable and sustainable manner. There are altogether 500 schools at different levels. The number of students exceeds 70,000. A fairly complete system from pre-school education and high school education to occupational education and higher education have been set up.

AFFORESTATION

In the 1990's, the afforestation area of Lhasa was 1359.88 hectares, accounting for 32% of the total area of the city. This greatly changed the old appearance of the city. In 1991, the Green Project of Lhasa was conferred the Praise of Excellent Comprehensive Administration by National Environmental Protection Bureau and Ministry of Construction.

Lhasa is developing into a tidy, nice garden city with beautiful scenery.

ORGANIZATIONS

Lhasa People's Congress: Lhasa People's Congress and its standing committee are the national power institutions in Lhasa. Its functions are examine and decide the major issues of the city, enhance the implementation of law and supervision of the work of the government, court and procuratorship, exercise the power of election, appointment and removal, supervision, decision, legislation, systemization and standardization.

People's Government of Lhasa Municipality

The People's Government of Lhasa Municipality is the implementing and executive body of Lhasa people's Congress. It is under the direct administration of the Government of Tibet Autonomous Region and is in charge of the executive work of the city.

FOREIGN RELATIONS

Since 1980's, Lhasa has been strengthening its reform and opening up and promoting crosswise economic combination. Achievements have been made in the work of invitation of bidding and attraction of investment. Now, Lhasa has twinned with 11 cities and regions abroad as Friendship Cities.

时 差 表

TIME

-7 柏林 BERLIN	+1 东京 TOKYO	-5 巴格达 BAGHDAD
-6 雅典 ATHENS	-0.30 雅加达 DJAKARTA	-7 巴黎 PARIS
-6 开罗 CAIRO	+1 汉城 SEOUL	-7 日内瓦 GENEVA
-1 曼谷 BANGKOK	-16 洛杉矶 Los Angeles	-8 伦敦 LONDON
-5 莫斯科 MOSCOW	-7 罗马 ROME	-13 纽约 NEWYORK
-5 科威特 KUWAIT	-13 多伦多 TORONTO	-2 悉尼 SYDNEY
-4.30 德黑兰 TEHRAN	+0.30 新加坡 Singapore	-3 卡拉奇 KARACHI

General Knowledge

HOW TO GO THROUGH THE FORMALITIES TO ENTER TIBET

If you plan to go to Lhasa for a visit or an investigation, please contact the Foreign Affairs Office of the People's Government of Lhasa Municipality and the Tourism Bureau of Lhasa Municipality for inquiry.
Tel: (0891)6324691, 6323632
Fax: (0891)6331175

In consideration of the infrastructure, the reception ability of transportation and tourism of Lhasa, the national cultural traditions of the Tibetan nationality, the culture relics, the natural environment and so on, the government encourages the development of group travel. All the foreigners who want to tour, go to visit their relatives, study, work or do business in Lhasa need to go through the formalities for an affirmation letter.

Affirmation Letter: All the tour groups from abroad need to arrange a confirmation letter through any international travel agency. Tibetan Tourism Bureau has set up branches at Beijing, Chengdu, Hong Kong, Kathmandu of Nepal to provide service for the tour groups.

Tibetan Autonomous Region Traveling-Tourist Bureau Office in Beijing
Tel: 010-65936538
Fax: 010-65936538

Office in Chengdu
Tel: 028-3401807
Fax: 028-3401807

Office in Hong Kong
Tel: 00852-29221028
Fax: 00852-25276337

Office in Nepal
Tel: 00977-1420964

Fax: 00977-1422758

Office in Shanghai
Tel: 021-62748488
Fax: 021-63211016

Office in Xi' an
Tel: 029-7815987
Fax: 029-7815987

Office in Guangzhou
Tel: 020-81099136
Fax: 020-81099136

Office in Chongqing
Tel: 023-65302750
Fax: 023-65302750

Office in Dalian
Tel: 0411-2646238
Fax: 0411-2646252

Office in Yunnan
Tel: 0887-8229028
Fax: 0887-8229028

Office in Shenzhen
Tel: 0755-5590159
Fax: 0755-5590160

Office in Ger' ermu
Tel: 0979-4835321
Tel: 0979-4835321

Office in Japan
Tel: 003-36393119
Fax: 003-36393896

Office in America
Tel: 001-9096298888
Fax: 001-9096298889

The Foreign Affairs Office of Tibet Autonomous Region takes the responsibility to receive diplomats and foreign reporters and handle the affirmation letters for them.

The Economic Bureau takes the responsibility to issue the affirmation letters for foreigners who conduct commercial activities.

The United Front Work Department takes the responsibility to receive the foreign Tibet compatriots who enter Tibet to visit relatives and issue the affirmation letters for them.

FLIGHT

There are flights from Beijing, Chengdu, Xi' an and Chongqing to Lhasa, and there is also an international flight from Lhasa to Kathmandu. There are two return flights from Chengdu to Lhasa a day and it takes about 2 hours one way.

AIRPORT

The airport is 97KM from downtown and it takes 50 to 80 minutes by car. You can pass by the Qushui Bridge, which is the longest bridge across River Yarlungzangbo and enjoy the natural scenery, and you can even park your car at Zhuoma Lakang for sightseeing.

FLIGHT TICKETS

Tickets can be booked at the flight tickets agencies or Dongga airport. Shuangliu airport at Chengdu also sells the tickets.

BUS

You can take shuttle buses with tourism signs from Chengdu, Xining or Ge Ermu to Lhasa and the journey normally takes 3-5 days. Sweaters should be prepared in summer and duck down coats should be prepared in winter.

MINI BUS

There are 8 mini bus routes radiating from downtown to suburbs. They can stop anywhere when you sign. The bus fare is 2 Yuan, or 3 Yuan after 9:00pm, some suburban routes cost 5 Yuan.

TAXIS

There are many taxis running through the city and the price is 10 Yuan, no matter where you go inside the city proper. Price can be discussed when you need to travel to the far suburbs.

RICKSHAW

Rickshaw is the supplementary travel tool in Lhasa. It is quite convenient for you to travel with luggage to a small street where the bus can not reach. The price is 3-10 Yuan.

BICYCLE

Most of the people in Lhasa go to work or go out by bikes. The roads in Lhasa are smooth and bicycle lanes are separated by green belt from the main road. But on narrow roads, lanes are kept for bicycles. Bikes can be rent by foreign guests at hotels.

LHASA POST OFFICE

Lhasa Post Office is the post and telecommunication center of Tibet Autonomous Region and it mainly deals with letters, packages, remittance, deposits and the publishing newspaper and magazines. Fast mailing, express mailing, stamp collection, telex and telephone service are also operated at this post office. The address of it is No. 64 Beijing Donglu Street, Lhasa.

LHASA TELECOMMUNICATION BUREAU

Lhasa Telecommunication Bureau is the telecommunication hub on Tibetan Plateau. Now the business in operation are telexes, phone calls inside the city, manual and direct dial long distance calls, cellular phone calls, magnetic phone calls, telephone meetings, television meetings. 126 beeper call service, 127 national automatic network beeper call service, 128 Chinese character beeper call service, 166 electronic voice box service, 168 phone information service, 112 automatic obstacle clearing service and 114 automatic number checking service. The address is No. 59 Linker Donglu, Lhasa.

MEDICAL SERVICE

There are many medical service organizations in Lhasa, including big hospitals and small clinics. You can get in touch with the following recommended hospitals when necessary.

People's Hospital of Tibet Autonomous Region
Add: North Linker Road, Lhasa
Tel: 6324883

No. 2 People's Hospital of Tibet Autonomous Region
Add: No. 8 East jiangsu Road, Lhasa
Tel: 6332462

Tibetan Hospital of Tibet Autonomous Region
Add: No. 14 Niangre Road, Lhasa
Tel: 6324883

General Hospital of Tibet Military Region
Add: Eorth Niangre Lu Beilu Road, Lhasa
Tel: 6323390

People's Hospital of Lhasa
Add: East Beijing Road, Lhasa
Tel: 6323212, 6323338

HEALTH PROTECTION KNOWLEDGE ON THE PLATEAU

The elevation of Lhasa is high, air pressure is low and the air is thin, the oxygen content in the air is only 68%. Sunshine is strong and lasts long. Its winter is long and very cold and there is no hot summer. The annual rainfall is small and it is especially dry in winter and spring. The climate on the plateau changes vertically obviously and the temperature differs tremendously from day to night. Most of the people have plateau symptoms when they first arrive, such as headache, short of breath, nausea, vomiting and

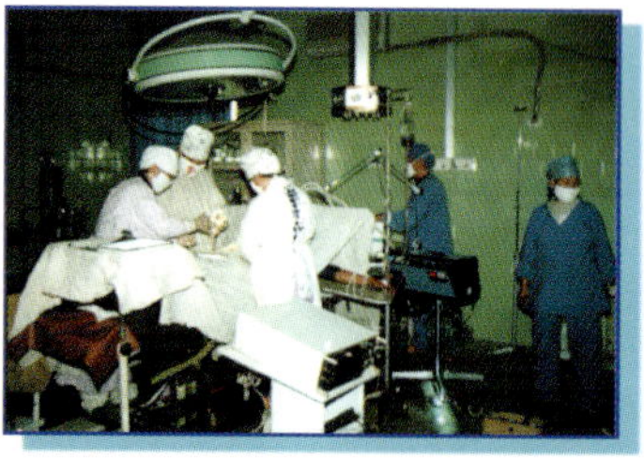

insomnia etc. At this time, violent activities should be banned, appropriate clothes should be worn and cold should be prevented. Usually the symptoms can be eased or disappear gradually in 2-3 days. However, serious heart and lung disease patients and patients with high blood pressure should better not travel on the plateau. The proper time to visit Tibet is from April to October. People should adjust themselves to the best health conditions before entering Tibet and traveling to Tibet should not be made when sick. Before taking the airplane, travelers should sleep enough and move slowly after taking off the plane. Heavy stuffs should not be lifted and deep breath should be made. Medicines such as tranquilizer and aminophylline could be taken according to the doctor' s advice. Take water soaked ginseng or keep it in the mouth are helpful to ease the plateau symptoms as well. If you are extremely short of oxygen, then you should breathe through the oxygen, then you should breathe through the oxygen bag (available at hotels and hospitals). If you catch a cold, you should have it cured in time so that it will not deteriorate to pulmonary emphysema. When going out, sunglasses and hat should be worn and sun proof oil should be used so as not to be scorched by sunshine. Food should not be overtaken when you first come, but vegetables, fruits and water should be largely taken in and smoking and drinking should be avoided.

CLOTHES

The characteristics of the climate at Lhasa is that the temperature at daytime and at night differ tremendously. Tourists who come to Lhasa in spring or fall should wear sweaters, but overcoat is needed in the morning and evening. The daytime at summer is fairly hot and a shirt is enough, but a sweater is needed in the morning and evening. The daytime in winter is warm, but a duck down jacket or cotton coat is needed in the morning and evening.

Tour and Sightseeing

Lhasa, the ancient city on the plateau, is an important city to the southwest border of China and the political, economic, cultural and religious center as well as the transportation hub in Tibet Autonomous Region. As the holy land of Tibetan Sect of Buddhism, Lhasa is one of the famous historical and cultural cities of China. It is included in the "List of World Cultural Relics" by UNESCO and well known for its long history, rich culture, unique traditions, a large number of cultural relics and strong relics and strong religious atmosphere. The number of historical places and holy land of Buddhism exceeds 200. There are about 20 scenic spots that have been developed and 30 that are being developed. Except the world famous Potala Palace and three major Monasteries of Yellow Sect of Buddhism, Jokhang Monastery, Ramoche Monastery and Norbu Lingka, there are also many ancient architectures, tombs, grottoes, statues, inscriptions on ancient bronze and stone tablets, cultural relics and historical sites. The splendid scenery at Nam Co Lake, the beautiful Damxung grassland, hot springs and gardens at Dezhong and natural protection zone at Maizhokunggar are all big attractions.

Lhasa attracts more and more visitors, climbers and scientists with its unique location, beautiful natural scenery, long history, rich culture, distinctive customs and many cultural relics and the unparalleled Buddhism features.

People of Lhasa warmly welcome the friends both from home and abroad to Lhasa for sightseeing.

Places of Worship

POTALA PALACE

Potala Palace is located at the center of the city and is one of the cultural relics that is under the national protection. The palace was constructed over 1300 years ago in the 7th century during Songtsan Gambo' s time. It is the largest and most complete castle construction group that still exists, and the place for pedigree of Dalai Lamas to conduct political affairs and live. It is also the power center of the unity of politics and religion in Tibet.

Potala Palace is an ancient monastery with the highest elevation. This construction at the top of Hongshan Mountain of ancient Lhasa has combined the essence of the arts of Tibetan and Han architecture. The height of this palace is 117.19 meters at an elevation of 3700 meters. It is 360 meters long from east to west and 270 meters wide from north to south, covering an area of 360,000 square meters.

Potala Palace is divided into two sections, the white palace and the red palace. The red palace is right in the center and the white palaces are on both sides. The building groups with white and red color compose a magnificent construction which is palace, castle as well as monastery.

JOKHANG MONASTERY

This construction is one of the cultural relics that is under the national protection designated by the State Council. It is one of the Tibetan famous monasteries, both well known at home and abroad. Songtsan Gambo had this built after he married Princess Wenchen from the Tang Dynasty and Princess Bhrikuti from Nepal in the middle of 7th Century. It has been renovated and expanded in the dynasties of the past 10 centuries and finally formed the current great construction group covering an area of 25,100 square meters. The whole construction has a unique style and looks magnificent. The gilded roof named Baoding and the high wall decorated with Dane create a holy place for pilgrims. The major building of Jokhang Monastery has 3 stories. If including the god halls at the four eaves of this building, there are 4 stories.

The more than 20 Halls, in which Sakyamuni are mainly worshiped, are full of statues made of gold, cooper and clay. The upper, middle and low corridors are painted with pictures describing various stories. These super construction art not only demonstrate the diligence of the Tibetan people, but also is a historical evidence of the friendly exchanges between Tibetan and Han people since ancient times.

DREPUNG MONASTERY

Situated at the col of Mt.

Ganpoi Uze in the western suburbs of Lhasa, which is 10KM from downtown, Drepung Monastery scatters all over the mountain by a large scale. When going inside, you' ll see it like a small town, tunnels run lengthwise and crosswise. This monastery, founded in 1416 by Jamyang Choje who was a famous disciple of Tsongkhapa, is one of the Three Major Monasteries of Yellow Sect.

Drepung Monastery is consisted of Assembly Hall, four colleges and Gandan pozhang, covering an area of 250,000 square meters. Inside the hall and outside the Sutra Hall golden top, Jinding, Xianglun, Baozhuang and Babao are adopted as decorations, which increase the solemn atmosphere of Buddhism and make the construction more magnificent. Drepung Monastery owns the largest construction scale and the largest number of lamas in the world.

SERA MONASTERY

The construction, covering an area of 115,000 square meters, is situated at the southern side of Sera Wuzi

Mountain at northern suburbs, which is 4KM away from downtown. It was built by Jamchen Choje, a disciple of Tsongkhapa in 1419 and the building is consisted of Assembly Hall, 3 colleges and 30 villages. The ceiling of Assembly hall is gilded in Xieshan style. Precious plate, pearl, Daozhuang, bird with man' s body are decorated at the roof of the building and Mojie fish head are put at the four eaves. Dougong of the inner land style under the gilded roof increase the religious atmosphere of the hall. This is one of the Three Major Monasteries of Yellow Sect.

GANDEN MONASTERY

Situated at the col of Mountain Wang Guer, southern bank of Lhasa River at Dagze County, Ganden Monastery was built by Tsongkhapa, creator of Gelugpa Sect (Yellow Sect) in 1409. It is regarded as the mother monastery of Gelugpa Sect and is the cultural relic under national protection. It is one of the Three Major Monasteries of Yellow Sect.

RAMOCHE MONASTERY

Ramoche Monastery was constructed in Lhasa and is located 500 meters to the north of Jokhang Monastery. The construction began in 647 and was completed at the same time Jokhang Monastery was finished. This Monastery faces the east, covering an area of 4000 square meters. Its front part is a courtyard and the back part is consisted of the hall for god and gate tower, as well as the auxiliary buildings, such as corridors. Ramoche Monastery is deeply respected by the Tibetan people.

NORBU LINGKA

Known as Jewel Garden, Norbu Lingka is a shining pearl of Lhasa. It is located in the west of the city and is the cultural relic under the national protection.

In 1755, which is the 20th year during Emperor Qianlong's reign, Kalsang Gyatso, the 7th Dalai, built this complex named Gesang Pozhang and used it as a summer resort. From April to September according to the Tibetan calendar, Dalai conducted political affairs and held various celebrations here. It had gradually become the summer palace for the pedigree of Dalai Lamas.

Norbu Lingka, like a museum, demonstrate to people the history, culture and art from different periods of Tibetan history.

REZHEN MONASTERY

Rezhen Monastery is the cultural relic under the protection of Tibet Autonomous Region. It is located at Guoxiang Town of Lhunzhub County and is one of the oldest monasteries of Tibet. In 1056, which was the beginning year of Emperor Jiayou of North Song Dynasty, Zhong Dunba, creator of the Gedang branch of Tibetan Buddhism built this compound. It is the first monastery of Gedang branch.

Rezhen Monastery relies on Mountain Yashan and faces running springs. Green trees are planted among the buildings with red walls and blue tiles. When fog rises in the beautiful mountain, you can be refreshed instantly. It is an ancient monastery that matches its fame.

CHUBU MONASTERY

Situated in Dolongdeqen county to the west of Lhasa, Chubu Monastery has Mt. Baima Qiongzong behind it. Trees flourish among the places. The Nengren Budda formed by nature vividly grow out of the mountain. It stands by the left side with a high breast and big belly. White cloud passes by the eastern part of the mountain and the western part of the mountain is like a Baidumu standing there Kamabaduisongqinba came here in 1159 and lived here to practice Buddhism for a long time, then he left for Kangdi and returned to Dolong at the age of 80 and established Chubu Monastery. Many cultural relics since Ming Dynasty are kept here.

LIULI BRIDGE

Situated 300 meters to the west of JoKhang Monastery at southern Yutuo Road. It used to be an important way connecting the inner and outer ancient Lhasa city. The bridge is made of stone and has 5 holes. The span is 28.3 meters and the width of the bridge is 6.8 meters. The stone walls are piled on both sides of the bridge and the wall is 1.6 meters thick and 3.2 meters high. The roof shaped like a upside down V and is covered with green glazed tiles. The four eaves are decorated with dragon heads, forming an outstanding bridge of ancient Han building in Xieshan style.

MONUMENT IN COMMEMORATION OF MEETING BETWEEN UNCLE AND NEPHEW FOR ALLIANCE AT CHANGQING:

This monument is beside the princess Willow in front of Jokhang Monastery. It is 4.78m high, 0.95m wide and 0.50m thick. The top is covered with a stone roof and the bottom is a stone turtle.

In 822 BC, the Tang Dynasty sent envoys to the capital of Tubo Dynasty. They not only had meetings with their counterparts and swore to form alliances, but also carved the oath on this stone monument and put it in front of Jokhang Monastery. This monument indicated the hope and willingness of both the Tibetan and Han people. What is more significant is that it is the important historical evidence of the long lasting friendship between Tibetan and Han people.

OUTER MONUMENT:

It's Tibetan name is "Dorenqima". Situated outside the gate of Potala Palace, it is symmetrical to another monument with no characters on it. Since it is at the bottom of the stairs connecting Potala, so it is called the outer monument.

This monument is also covered with a stone roof and carved with Tibet letters on three sides, the other side is empty. It is the oldest monument that has been discovered so far in the Tibetan Autonomous Region. During Chisong Desan's time, he read personally imperial edict of the oath of alliance and ordered to set up this monument in order to praise his Minister of Internal Affairs, Dazha Lugong.

UNDERGROUND HEAT RESOURCES AT YANG BAJING:

The underground heat resources are rich in Lhasa and the underground steam field at Yang Bajing is the most famous one. It' s in Damxung County and covers 7,700 square meters. The temperature can be maintained at 47 degrees centigrade. It is the underground heat electricity generating station with the highest elevation in the world and is also the first steam field that has been developed in the mainland of China.

There is a hot-lake which is 16 meters deep in the northeast steam field. The lake is blue and the hot water bubbles furiously. The temperature of

lake ranges from 47 to 59 degrees centigrade. Bathrooms are built by the lake, so people can have a comfortable tepid bath.

The steam field of Yang Bajing which is steaming all the time lie in the embrace of the snow-covered mountains. This perfect combination constitutes a natural wonder on the Roof of the World.

DEZHONG HOT SPRING

It is located in the Dezhong, Menba District of Maizhokunggar County that is over 4300 meters above sea level. The temperature of the hot spring is 42 Cels., and the rate of flow is 68 liters per second. The hot spring has many special curative effects and is crowned as the No. 1 hot spring in the world by the experts from the United States, Germany, Japan and so on.

NAM CO LAKE

Located in the Damxug County, Lhasa. It means "the heavenly lake" or "the god lake". The lake attracts lots of believers to pilgrim here from far away.

The lake is deep and blue,

which produces the fish without scale and with slim scale. Every summer, flocks of water fowls perch in the broad lake sides and the island in the center of the lake. The broad lake sides are rich in grass, so many animals haunt here. It is an excellent natural farm.

The blue lake and the snow-white mountain contrast finely with each other, consisting of the most beautiful natural landscape in Tibet.

BAGUOJIE STREET

It is the most prosperous circle-shaped commercial street which is built around Jokhang Temple. It mostly sells light industry products and handicrafts with strong national characteristics that are produced in Tibet, India and Nepal. This is also the most important road for the Tibetan followers of Buddhism to transfer the Scripture.

THE POTALA PALACE SQUARE

The Potala Palace Square, located in the center of Lhasa City, is the very place where many important events are held by the Autonomous Region. In 1995, the ceremony celebrating the 30th anniversary of the foundation of the Tibet Autonomous Region was held here. This was the first time that it was used after the square was completed.

The imposing Potala Palace stands tall and upright in the very front of the Square. There is a big lotus fountain with strong national characteristics in the center of the square.

During holidays, flag-raising ceremony is held here. The whole square basks in the beautiful sunshine, the fountain is colorful and the lights are brilliant. It is one of the most favorite places that the citizens and tourists would like to visit.

HOLY LAKE MADE BY MAN

Dragon King Pond is a famous garden architecture in Tibetan Zongjiaolukan garden. It is a man-made lake from digging when the 5th Dalai rebuilt Potala Palace in 17th Century. Later 6th Dalai set up a 3-storey building named Dragon King Palace in the hill at the center of the lake. So it's called Dragon King Pond.

Traditions and Customs

Lhasa is the place where many ethnic groups are inhabited and the major nationality here is Tibetan. Tibetans have their own language and usually believe in Buddhism. Religion has been permeated though social field as a cultural phenomenon and produces extensive and profound influence to people' s life, production and entertainment. Tibetans have no surnames, and the given names normally have 2 or 4 characters and mainly mean auspicious. Tibetans have a bold and straightforward character and are good at singing and dancing. The region is nicknamed the sea of songs and dances. The Tibetan nationality has formed a unique humanity landscape with its rich traditional entertainment, special dress, personal adornment, food and drink, and folk living, marriage and funeral customs.

People of Lhasa are simple, honest and unspoiled and warm-hearted to show the way for the tourist.

LANGUAGE

Tibetans speak Tibetan language, but most of them can speak fluent Mandarin. They decide to use the equivalent language according to their conversational partner. Explanations in Mandarin and Tibetan can be found at hotels, restaurants and shops. However, it is better for foreign tourists to go out in groups with interpreters accompanying The domestic tourists can go anywhere without problems. People of Lhasa are very unsophisticated and helpful to give directions for people.

CLOTHES

Long sleeves, wide waist and front of garment are the characteristics of the traditional clothes of Tibetans. Cotton print and silk are usually decorated at collar, sleeves, front and bottom of the garment. In mountainous areas, clothes are usually made of felt, wool and cotton. Women' s clothes have no sleeves and are worn together with colorful shirt

and apron. In farming area, the major material of clothes are various leathers and the clothes are looser.

FOOD

The traditional food and drink of Tibetans are roasted Qingke barley flour, flour, dried meat, beef and mutton eating with hand, milchig, butter tea, sweet tea and barley wine, etc.

HOUSING

The stone or wooden-structured houses with flat roof are the major residential buildings for the rural Tibetans. The buildings have 2 or 3 stories and are decorated with corridors inside the courtyards. The rooms are decorated with nicely carved furniture in Tibetan style and other ornament. In farming areas, people live in tents made of cloth or leather.

TRADITIONAL FESTIVALS

The Tibetan people celebrate their colorful and special festivals which have a heavy tone of religion. With time passing by, those festivals keep the original contents but more entertainments are added, presenting a fresh ground.

HANDCRAFTS INDUSTRY

The handcrafts industry enjoys a long history, which is like a bright pearl in the treasure house of arts of the Chinese nationalities. Besides the traditional felt, carpet, apron and knife, there are also quilt, dress, boot, hat, cushion, wooden bowl, pottery and metal crafts with distinguish Tibetan features.

The handcrafts industry in Lhasa has set up a bridge among

the peoples of all nationalities and developed their friendship.

SHOPPING

Commercial networks in Lhasa are constantly increasing and there are 8 major shopping places. People prefer to go to the following markets:

Barkhor Market

It mainly sells agriculture by-products, daily used commodities, garments and shoes.

Lhasa Trade Mall

It sells general merchandise, home appliances, food, knitting products, sports products, cosmetics and fold arts and crafts.

Qing Nianlu Market

It is a garment street and mainly deals with garments.

Apart from the above shopping places, you can also do your shopping at other shopping places that scatter across the city.

TELEPHONE NUMBER
电 话 号 码 表

TELEPHONE NUMBER
拉萨市电话号码表

拉萨市公安局办公室 6322858
西藏自治区公安厅外管处 6330221-4095

拉萨市外事服务单位

拉萨饭店 6832221
民族路1号
西藏宾馆 6834966
北京西路221号
日光宾馆 6322227
林聚路27号
西藏大厦 6826091
北京中路196号
迎宾馆 6322184
宇拓路34号
八郎学宾馆 6323829
北京中路43号
吉日旅馆 6323462
北京中路105号
哈达旅馆 6323430
江苏路23号
亚宾馆 6323496
北京东路100号
雪域宾馆 6323687
藏医院路4号
高原宾馆 6326084
当热路
金谷饭店 6330357
宇拓路14号
嘎吉林宾馆 6326685
团结新村
白云宾馆 6826096
北京中路196号
藏北大厦 6813736
娘热路17号
大吉酒店 6337777
林廓东路34号
新世纪宾馆 6334895
北京东路155号
航空酒店 6833444
康昂东路14号
岗坚拉萨饭店 6337666
北京东路83号
乐吉林餐饮公司 6829154
北京中路181号
区纪检培训中心 6324539
宇拓路71号
区组织培训中心 6835720
娘热路1号
机场宾馆 6182243
贡嘎机场
诺达康桑宾馆 6341737
色拉路168号
香巴拉饭店 6323888
丹杰路1号
山水宾馆 6348686
北京中路29号
天湖宾馆 6112098
当雄县当曲镇文化馆

和平饭店 6330888
江苏路10号
达氏宾馆 6344888
小昭寺路15号
商业宾馆 6325888
康昂东路8号
邮政酒店 6821999
北京东路33号
扎西达杰宾馆 6325804
藏医院路8号
满斋酒店 6338940
八廓南街
攀多旅馆 6330700
藏医东路5号
琅赛宾馆 6329651
当热路
雄巴拉大酒店 6338888
江苏路28号
敦固宾馆 6322555
夏萨苏德吉路19号
天河宾馆 6338138
宇拓路
天域交通宾馆 6822828
罗布林卡路4号
西藏虹侨宾馆 6320088
北京东路161号
巴扎旅馆 6325580
林廓东路48号
吉曲宾馆 6338824
北京东路149号
凯拉斯酒店 6340904
北京东路143号

西藏自治区国际旅行社

西藏旅游总公司 6836626
拉萨北京西路208号
拉萨市旅游公司 6337237
拉萨林聚路27号
西藏日喀则国旅 6834966-104
西藏宾馆104房
西藏山南国旅 6834324
北京西路208号
西藏体育旅游公司 6334082
拉萨林廓东路6号
西藏神山旅行社 6826096-1113
西藏大厦1113号
西藏职工旅行社 6823664
北京西路215号
西藏青年旅行社 6326451
拉萨金珠东路31号
西藏龙达旅行社 6833009
拉萨北京西路208号
西藏那曲旅游公司 6328851
拉萨北京东路16号
西藏茶马古道国际旅行社 6813564
北京西路170号
西藏港珠旅行社 6836863
拉萨园林路18号
西藏假日旅行社 6324305
拉萨民族路1号
西藏科技国际旅行社 6830767
北京西路230号
西藏尼威国际旅行社 6336375
林廓北路12号

西藏世纪国际旅行社 6836887
北京西路221号
西藏亚克国际旅行社 6839306
北京中路180号
西藏山水国际旅行社 6333829
北京东路132号
西藏航空国际旅行社 6833331
康昂东路14号
西藏圣洁导游服务中心 6829226
北京西路208号
西藏高原散客管理接待中心 6349239

西藏自治区国内旅行社

西藏亚龙旅行社 6835182
民族路10号
林芝香巴拉旅行社 6320177
北京东路131号
拉萨电信旅行社 6336898
林廓东路59号
西藏金谷旅行社 6330367
宇拓路14号
电力腾飞旅游有限公司 6341603
娘热路245号
西藏布达拉民间旅行社 6329034
北京东路
西藏环宇旅行社 6833879
北京中路184号
西藏外事服务中心 6335051
林廓北路
神湖旅行社 010-64980389
北京中路198号
乌孜旅行社 6322777
夺底路26-1号
泽当电信雪鸽旅行社 13980006788
山南泽当湖北路
西藏藏康康藏旅行社 08054-2224
昌都芒康县嘎拖镇
西藏喜雅旅行社 6828257
北京中路59号
西藏邮电旅行社 6322824
林廓东路1巷5号
西藏藏之旅旅行社有限公司
宇拓路18号 13908913466
西藏玛旁雍错旅行社 13908973408
阿里普兰县贡嘎路

餐 饮 娱 乐

石头屋餐厅 6321627
布达拉宫销售楼
尼威格桑花大酒楼 6336648
林廓北路
八廓咖啡厅 6326892
八角西街20号
圣城餐厅 6826756
北京西路38号
羌塘怪牛餐厅 6331999
轻纺贸易公司院内
雪神宫藏式餐厅 6335866
布达拉宫广场西侧
雪域旅馆餐厅
藏医院路4号
阿波罗酒庄 6814955
民族北路